About the Author

David is married with three grown-up children and two grandchildren, and lives on the Isle of Wight. He used to run a musical instrument repair business from home, but now he writes full-time. His hobbies are gardening, playing musical instruments, song writing and composing poetry.

He has been writing songs and poems for as long as he can remember, but it had not occurred to him to write for children until his eldest daughter suggested that, perhaps, he should have a go, and with further encouragement from friends and family, this is the result.

Acknowledgements

I would like to thank my wife, family and friends for their kind help and encouragement in compiling this book of poems, which has been written for children of all ages. I wish to acknowledge that it was mostly my family who gave me the ideas for these poems.

I would also like to thank Christian Hennessey for his humorous illustrations for each of the poems.

I wish to dedicate this book to my younger brother and sister, Peter and Heidi, who are sadly no longer with us.

Grandma's Roller Skates
and Other Silly Poems

by

David A. Ballard

Illustrated by
Christian Hennessey

Beachy Books

www.beachybooks.com

For my friends and family with their encouragement and support
and my grandchildren, Jude and Erin, for their ongoing inspiration.

First published by Beachy Books in 2017
www.beachybooks.com

1 2 3 4 5 6 7 8 9 10

British Library Cataloguing in Publication Data.
A catalogue record for this book is available from the British Library.

ISBN: 9781999728304
Design and typesetting by Philip Bell (Beachy Books)
Set in HanziPen SC

Contents

A Cat Named Boofs

I'm a cat who knows where it's at.
Myself I'll introduce.
My name's a bit unusual,
but I'm mostly known as Boofs.

I am beautiful they tell me,
but I'm really rather vain.
I like to preen my nice fur coat.
That's how I got my name.

My favourite hobby's eating –
and my attitude?
I don't care where it comes from,
as long as it is food!

My other hobby's sleeping
and I often dream
of fish cakes, prawns or liver
and a nice big dish of cream.

I'm always feeling hungry,
and, if I had my way,
I'd have my lunch and dinner
at least six times a day.

I go round to visit neighbours
for that extra meal
and now and then lay on their bed,
depends on how I feel.

I somehow sneak in quietly,
in the hope that I'm not seen,
and if there's food to find there
I'll lick the platter clean.

All this can be quite tiring
so I have to rest my head,
find a sofa to lie down on,
or somebody's bed.

I don't know when you'll see me,
but I turn up now and then.
Just put something in my food bowl
and I will be your friend.

Lots of love
Boofs (Beautiful)

A Change of Plan

Oh, what a shame
it's started to rain,
I was going to play with some friends.
Now I'm stuck here indoors
and getting quite bored,
my plans have come to an end.

But I don't want to play
indoors all day.
I could be out and about on my bike.
There's no other way
so here I must stay
resolved to this unfortunate plight.

Mum rescues me
and says how would it be
if we had a really good bake.
In the end it was fun,
we made some nice buns,
some bread, some pizza and cake.

Then Mum and me
had some for tea.
The pizza was really delicious.
I enjoyed the whole day,
but I just have to say,
I didn't like doing the dishes.

A Musical Talent

There's a boy in our class with a talent,
one that I'd like to describe,
for he is musically gifted,
it's a gift he dispels with great pride.
Now some people like playing a trumpet,
others may bang on a drum.
The lad in our class though is different,
he plays a tune with his bum.

He'll play any request that you ask for;
he has a large repertoire
and he will often keep going.
It's a wonder his bum's not on fire.
He will willingly play Happy Birthday
or any song straight from the charts.
He'll play the National Anthem
with a string of nice tuneful farts.

The teachers don't think it's so funny.
He often gets sent out of class.
They say that it's rather disruptive
and we can't get on with our task,
but I think I'd much rather hear him
playing a nice little tune,
though sometimes it can be rather smelly,
so it's us who must leave the room.

This talent is quite entertaining
and really sets him apart.
Sometimes he's just showing off though,
like when he was playing Mozart.
Maybe he'll join the wind section
of the orchestra here in our school.
We could all go to the concert,
now that would really be cool.

He says he wants to be famous,
well maybe he will be one day,
though I find that hard to imagine
him doing his own cabaret.
You can picture him there in the theatre
with the audience all singing along.
Maybe they might just enjoy it,
as long as they don't mind the pong!

A Clown

When I grow up I want to be
a funny circus clown
with one of those red noses
so I can act and fool around.
I'll get my face all painted
and have big extended feet,
make people laugh
so much that they
will fall out of their seats.

I'll get myself the outfit,
baggy trousers, hat and coat,
do funny mimes and sketches
and lots of silly jokes.
I'll get out my diablo
and learn to juggle things.
I know that I will love it
in the circus ring.

I'll get a car that falls apart,
you know the one I mean.
Or a ladder that collapses –
have I set the scene?
I can just imagine,
the roaring of the crowd.
To be a clown when I grow up,
that's if I'm allowed.

I can think of nothing better
than making people laugh.
To watch the tears
roll down their faces
and cheer them up.   Not half.
There is something really special
when the circus comes to town.
That's why I would like to be
a funny circus clown.

An Imaginary Friend

My sister's kind of weird you know.
It drives me round the bend.
She has a strange fixation,
an imaginary friend.

We have to go along with it.
I don't see why I should.
It all seems rather stupid.
It won't do any good.

Mum lays a place at the table,
when we have a meal,
for this imaginary person
pretending they are real...

There's even conversation.
"Would you like some sauce?"
They never get an answer.
There's no one there of course.

When we're watching telly
I'm told "You can't sit there!"
so I sit on the floor because
that's her best friend's chair.

When it comes to Christmas
it really puzzles me;
there are imaginary presents
underneath the tree.

Is everybody bonkers?
Has no one got a brain?
It seems to me that this whole thing
is really quite insane.

I really can't imagine why
she likes this friend the most?
The only explanation is
this person is a ghost.

Back Street International

There's a small plot of land
at the end of our street
where the boys around here
all like to meet.
We don't do anything naughty,
just kick a ball around
and we all like to think
we're the best team in town.

We like to pretend that
we'll play for the cup
and when the game's over,
we're covered in muck.
Then on home we'd go,
what a sight to be seen.
It's a good job that Mum's
got a washing machine.

One or two parents
come and watch, now and then.
We all know each other
for these lads are my friends.
We may not be professionals
like some famous names.
Our reason for playing is
we just like the game.

When I grow up
it's my great big dream
to be a professional
and play in a team.
Perhaps I'll be famous
and earn lots of dosh
and be just like Beckham
and be married to Posh.

Bedtime Story

Read me a bedtime story,
tell me a tale or two.
The one about three little piggies
or something from Winnie The Pooh.

Make sure the ending is happy.
I don't like stories too sad.
And when you have finished with that one,
read me another please, Dad!

I'd like to see all the pictures
so sit on the edge of the bed.
We'll follow the pictures together.
That's how a book should be read.

Tell me a tale of King Arthur,
about all his knights so bold,
of Lancelot, Gwenevere, Merlin
and a sword in a stone, so I'm told.

Do you know one about pirates
who sailed on the Spanish Main?
With ships full of sail on the high seas
and of the treasures they gain.

Tell me a story that's funny
so the tears just roll down my cheeks
and I grow exhausted with laughter
'till eventually I fall asleep.

Bernie the Bookworm

Now Bernie the Bookworm is a remarkable creature.
In any old book you'll see him feature,
chomping his way and thinking he's clever
through paperbacks, hardbacks and some bound in leather.

He does not like burgers or chips cooked in batter,
it's the pages of books that make him fatter.
From breakfast to dinner he continues to munch on
all sorts of books are his kind of luncheon.

He reads lots of books on adventure and travel,
Sherlock Holmes mysteries he likes to unravel.
Romantic stories where the boy gets the girl,
or science fiction adventures that are out of this world.

He likes a whodunit like Agatha Christie,
or a thriller with plots complicated and twisty.
Tales that are sad or ones that are funny.
All of them eventually end up in his tummy.

He will chew his way through a whole range of subjects,
from Winnie The Pooh to plays such as Hamlet.
History, nature and poetry too,
books on philosophy, he'd plough his way through.

Autobiographies, nature or science,
to every subject that same keen appliance,
but with all of this knowledge you would have to agree
he should go to college and get a degree.

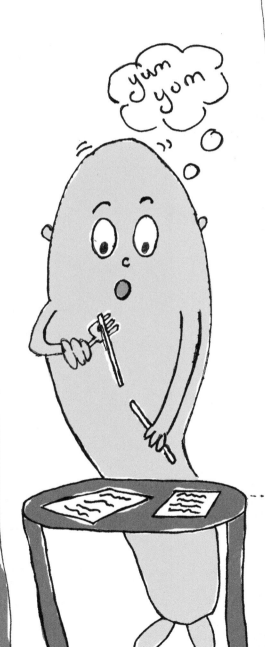

Biscuit Tree

Mummy and Daddy laughed at me.
I suggested we planted a biscuit tree.
What's wrong with that? Don't you agree?
Why can't I plant a biscuit tree?

Dad planted some grapes, though they took some time,
now they are big and they look just fine.
He uses the grapes for making some wine.
What's wrong with a biscuit tree?

He planted potatoes into the ground.
Later that summer he dug up and found
that one potato grew into several pounds.
What's wrong with a biscuit tree?

Many other things my dad has sown,
various edible things he has grown.
Surely it can't be that unknown
to grow a biscuit tree?

If we could grow biscuits that would be great.
When you think of the quantity that we all ate
there would always be enough to put on your plate.
What's wrong with a biscuit tree?

Chocolate chip cookies, digestives, cream puffs,
with a tree in the garden that would be more than enough.
I am sure it can not really be all that tough
to grow a biscuit tree.

Gingernuts, Shortbread and Bourbons there'd be,
the great thing is that they'd all be free.
You could come round and have some for tea
from my little biscuit tree.

Think of the money that Mummy would save
whenever for biscuits we would all crave
and solving world hunger a good idea made
by planting a biscuit tree.

Catching Tadpoles

Catching tadpoles
from a pond
is an occupation
of which I'm fond.
All you need's
a jar and a net.
You'll be surprised
the amount you will get.

Throw in the breadcrumbs
to use as a bait.
Hold the net
and then just wait.
When around the bread
the tadpoles will swim.
Just lift the net
and scoop them in.

Take them home
inside your jar
so friends and family
can see, admire.
There is one little drawback.
No one can stop it
when they turn to frogs –
watch out, they'll hop it!

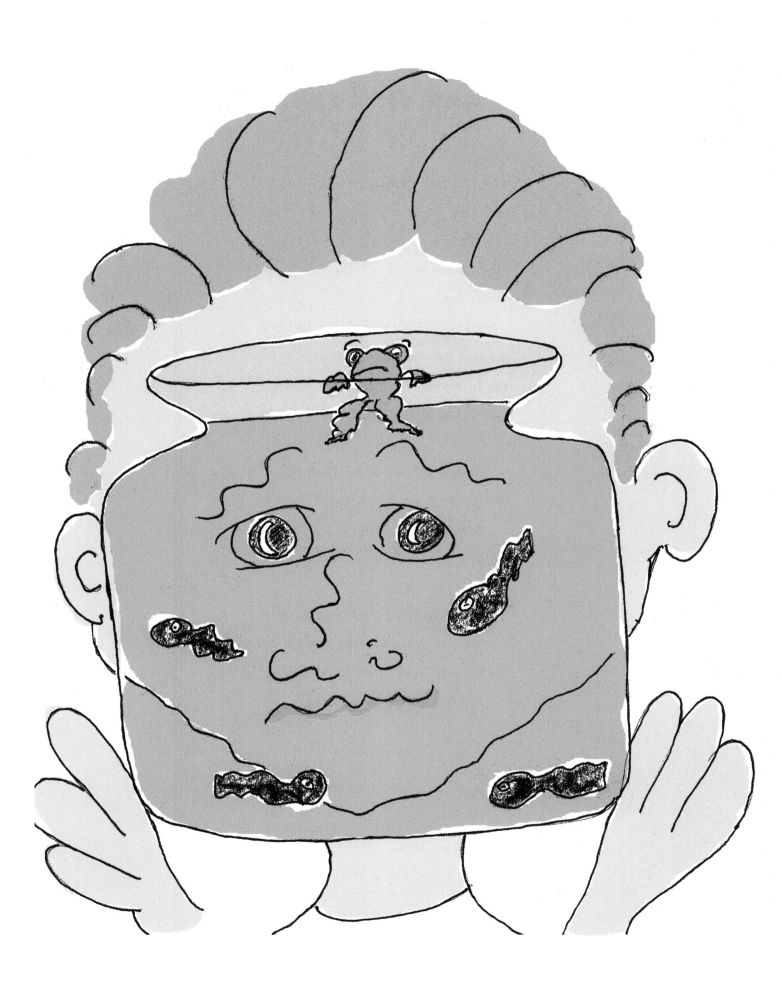

End of Term

The school term's nearly over
and the year comes to an end.
Say goodbye to all the lessons,
the teachers and our friends.

Now we let our hair down
as we go our separate ways;
each of us, in turn, it seems,
making plans and holidays.

Some of us are leaving
and won't be back next term;
others going up a class,
more lessons to be learned.

So let's say all our farewells
as we go out the gate.
Until we meet up next term,
let's enjoy the break.

Feeling Poorly

The doctor said,
"You must stay in bed,
this may be slightly contagious.
I'm afraid that you've got
what we call chicken pox.
To get rid of it simply takes ages.
Just as I supposed
the thermometer shows
your temperature's a little unsteady,
so if I were you,
the thing I would do
is snuggle down with your teddy."

So my mum gave to me
some nice T.L.C
and hot water bottles to warm up my belly.
I laid there and looked
at a couple of books
and sometimes some programmes on telly.
I don't mind at all
if it means missing school
however long it may take.
It's so nice to stay
in bed every day.
That is until I'm back in shape.

Giggling Gertie

Giggling Gertie
had a laugh, oh so dirty –
she would cackle away like a hen.
Tell her a joke
and with just one stroke
she would fall around laughing again.

Her eyes filled with mirth
and her rather large girth
would wobble around like a jelly.
Her humour was such
that she'd laugh so much
she would have to hold on to her belly.

She's a happy old soul,
life with her's never dull.
She will lift up your spirits I've found
if you need cheering up
or are down on your luck.
What a great woman to have around.

It seems to me
that there's bound to be
someone you know of like that.
Her laugh is outrageous,
she's simply contagious,
she will laugh at the drop of a hat.

Grandad's Lost His Marbles

Grandad's lost his marbles
I heard my grandma say.
She was talking to my mummy;
I heard them yesterday.
They whispered to each other
thinking that I couldn't hear,
but they had no explanation
why Grandad's marbles should disappear.

I could lend him mine though,
I got lots and lots.
I keep them in my bedroom
in a wooden box.
So if he's lost his marbles
he might like some of mine.
I'd gladly lend them to him.
I'm sure that would be fine.

Maybe I could help him
find the marbles that he's lost.
We could buy some new ones;
there's no need to make a fuss.
I cannot understand,
it doesn't make much sense.
Let's go down the toy shop –
they only cost 50 pence!

People often lose their marbles,
that's what I was told
and it sometimes happens
to someone when they're old.
The grown-ups started laughing
when I told them of my plan.
It's not that kind of marbles,
pointed out my gran.

Grandma Had a Game of Darts

Grandma had a game of darts.
Her aim was very poor.
One dart hit the mantelpiece,
another hit the floor.
One stuck on the ceiling,
one fell on the mat.
The worst thing that my grandma did
was nearly hit the cat.

I won't put money on it,
but I'm inclined to bet,
in spite of all her efforts,
she's not hit the dartboard yet.
We told her to stand nearer.
It might improve her aim.
I'm sad to say that anyway
the results were all the same.

Perhaps if it was bigger;
her aim is rather wide.
For every time she throws one
we all run and hide.
We'll do it in the garden.
That's a good idea,
but she lost them in the flower bed.
It's getting worse I fear.

We took her to the Hare and Hounds,
the dart team's very good.
She might learn a thing or two,
at least I understood.
My dad gave her some lessons
and how to flick her wrist,
he bought my gran a glass of wine
and some cheese and onion crisps.

After several lessons
and quite a bit of wine
she stood there in position,
her feet upon the line.
Eyes fixed upon the dartboard,
she looked so self-assured
and went and scored a bullseye
in the middle of the board.

Since then she's been improving,
it must have been the wine,
for Grandma's in the dartboard team
and now she's doing fine.
They play in lots of matches;
there are several leagues around.
She's even won a game or two
in this new hobby that she's found.

Grandma's Roller Skates

Grandma bought some roller skates;
you should have seen her going.
Where she went and got them
I've no way of knowing.
She'd go up and down the high street
dodging cars and buses,
but blissfully quite unaware
of just what all the fuss is.

She went into a supermarket
to do a little shopping.
Once inside, those nice clean floors
she found there was no stopping.
Causing lots of havoc,
among the special offers,
she collided with the baked beans
and nearly came a cropper.

The crash was quite a big one,
heard throughout the store.
Some thought that a bomb went off
and headed for the door.
Grandma laid upon her back,
her legs up in the air
and all the people passing by
could see her underwear.

Grandma learnt her lesson
with her roller skates.
The thing she did not realise,
they don't have any brakes.
"One thing that I am sure of"
I heard my Grandma twitter.
"I'm so glad upon that day
that I was wearing knickers!"

Hamster

I lost my little hamster,
it was really rather sad,
because he was the bestest hamster
anybody ever had.
His light brown fluffy overcoat,
his whiskers oh so long.
Now, I can't believe
that my little hamster's gone.

The last time that I saw him
was before I went to bed.
Next thing I know this morning
the little thing is dead.
Can anybody tell me,
is there anyone who knows,
seems as if a light went out,
where do dead things go?

He really was no trouble.
He never did no harm.
Sometimes I'd let him out and he'd
run up and down my arm.
His cage had all it needed,
a wheel, a bowl, some straw.
I just can't believe that I
won't see him anymore.

A funeral tomorrow.
Mum says it's for the best.
He was getting rather old so now
we'll lay him down to rest.
The family will be there.
I'm glad they share my loss.
We will say a little prayer for him
and plant a little cross.

Home

Home is where the heart is
you often hear folks say.
A place to come home to
at the end of every day.

Somewhere to escape to,
from the daily grind,
a sanctuary, oasis,
a place you can unwind.

You shut the door behind you
and leave the world outside.
The fox, the rabbit and the mouse
all need a place to hide.

Be it cave or castle,
it's worthwhile to invest.
Everybody needs to
have a little nest.

Insight

I saw this gorgeous sunset
as I came home last night.
I stood a while and watched it;
it was such a lovely sight.
Just then I saw this woman,
someone that I knew.
She stopped a while to talk to me.
I said, "How do you do?"
She could not see the sunset
and it crossed my mind
there are many things that one could miss
if, like Tina, you were blind.
Now if I was a poet,
maybe I could try
to paint a picture with some words
of those patterns in the sky.
How would I describe it?
I would not have a clue.
I do not have the means it seems
to convey that point of view.
And as I continued walking,
it's then I realised,
there's so much we take for granted,
but Tina has no eyes.

Litterbugs

No one loves a litterbug.
They just don't seem to care.
They have this awful habit
of leaving litter everywhere.
Wrappers, bottles, cartons,
paper, packets, tins.
I just don't understand it –
have they not heard of bins?
And if they cannot find one,
still that's no excuse.
They could put it in their pocket;
it's rubbish to refuse.

No one loves a litterbug.
It makes the place untidy.
You can put out all your rubbish
coz the dustman comes on Friday.
If we picked up all our litter
and it's something to be seen.
If everybody did this
our streets would all be clean.
So come on all you litterbugs,
please bear it in mind,
leave the place the same way
as you'd like to find.

Loitering Intent

Let's pitch a tent in the garden;
we'll find a nice piece of ground.
I will ask my mum and dad nicely
if they'd let some friends come round.

We can stay up till midnight,
cook some bangers and beans,
have a feast full of chocolate,
and finish off with ice cream.

I hope there are no scary monsters
who creep around in the night,
dancing around in the shadows
and giving everybody a fright.

I know we will have lots of fun though,
in our tent camped out on the lawn.
We will talk the hind legs off a donkey
and won't get to sleep until dawn.

I am sure if I asked them nicely
my parents will say that it's fine.
After all, it will soon be my birthday
and I will be thirty nine.

My Ambition

When I leave school I want to be
a famous person on T.V.
A well known star, a celebrity.
That is my ambition.
I don't want to be obscure,
in a job I find a bore
and not be heard of anymore.
Just one more addition.

Everywhere I will be seen
driving in my limousine.
I'll be the cat that got the cream,
a man for every season.
I'll spend my money I suppose
on lots of nice things,
cars and clothes
and my bank book overflows.
I will never need a reason.

You'll hear about me in the news
or maybe doing interviews.
Go out with any girl I choose,
a well known man of fashion.
I'll buy a house
that's somewhere warm,
have parties that go on till dawn
with empty bottles on the lawn.
I'll live my life with passion.

But it's a dream I can't fulfill;
I somehow think I never will.
I must swallow this bitter pill.
Goodbye to that adventure.
For there's a problem, one small thing,
some kind of talent I should bring,
but I can neither dance nor sing.
I'm off down the Job Centre.

My Birthday

Today is my birthday.
I cannot wait
for the sound of the postman
as he comes through the gate.
Hope he brings presents
and cards by the score.
Oh, hurry up postman,
I cannot wait anymore.

Some will have money
that relatives send
or maybe one or two
sent from a friend.
They will go on the mantelpiece,
all in a row.
Oh, hurry up postman,
don't be so slow!

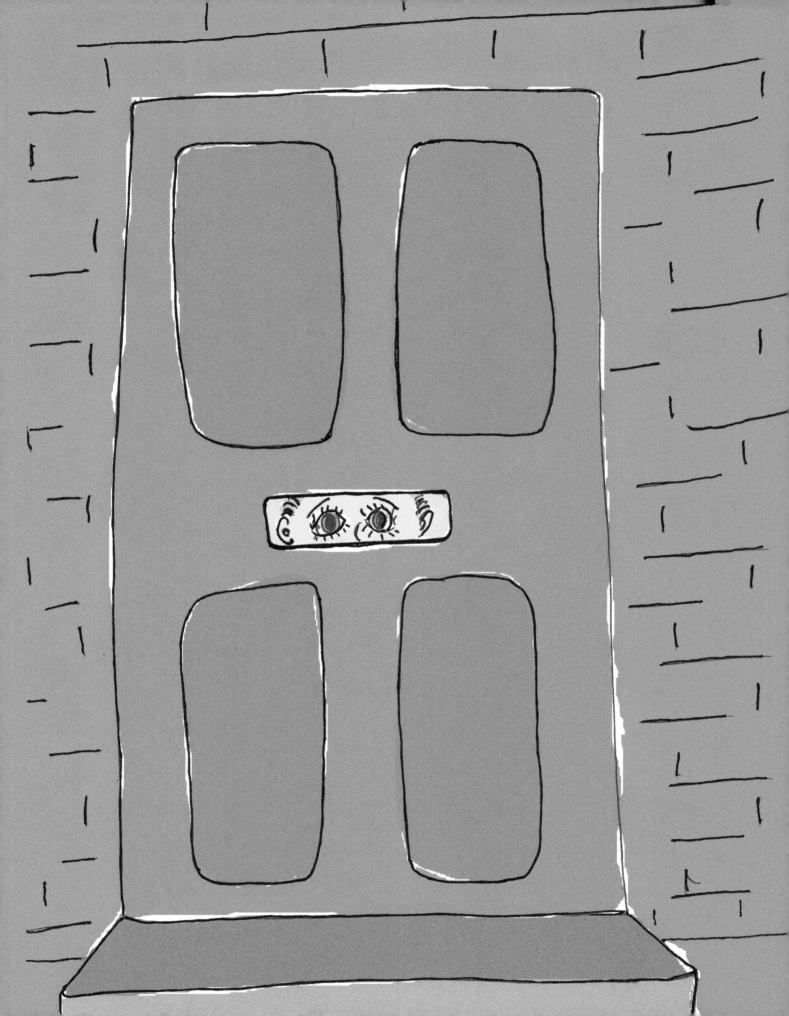

My Dad and His Wig

Dad went and bought a wig today.
It really looks so funny.
I don't understand it
and neither does my mummy.
It looks kind of silly
but it covers up his patch.
It reminds me of some old straw
on houses that are thatched.

I can't take my eyes of it
no matter how I try.
The next door neighbour
laughed so much
it almost made him cry.
You see Dad's got this parting
that's really very wide
and the reason that he bought a wig
was to cover up his pride.

He thinks no one will notice it
now he's got some hair.
When really if the truth be known
there is nothing there.
He's not fooling anybody
I know, I heard them say,
for there's an old expression –
toupée or not toupée.

It's quite unnecessary;
he could have bought a hat.
When he sat down on the sofa
he frightened off the cat.
The situation's out of hand,
it's getting rather sticky.
After all he is my dad
and we shouldn't take the
mickey.

My Grandad's Shed

Have I ever said about my grandfather's shed?
It's a place I'd like to describe.
Sometimes I would go and Grandad would show
what he was doing inside.

You'd see he likes woodwork, he made lots of things.
He utilised all kinds of wood
with walnut or oak, something bespoke
and always it looked very good.

An Aladdin's cave, with its sawdust and lathe
and the smell of shellac and wax.
In the corner there stood some odd planks of wood
and tools held neatly in racks.

Chisels in rows with dust interposed.
There were saws with nice sharpened teeth
and what is more, there was a bandsaw
and a workbench with cupboards beneath.

Grandad spent his time, come rain or shine,
making something or other.
One time I recall in no time at all
we made something for my little brother.

It was a small toy just right for a boy
who's birthday came in November.
And sometimes you know he'd let me have a go.
It's something I'll always remember.

That cedar or pine, it stays in my mind,
a smell I have come to adore.
I remember so well, that old workshop smell
each time I opened the door.

My grandfather has gone, but his memory lives on
here inside my head.
I'd have to agree it made an impression on me,
my grandfather's old wooden shed.

My Kite

Flying my kite, what a beautiful sight
on an October afternoon.
I pull the string as it catches the wind
and sails like a small balloon.

The wind takes a hold as it starts to unfold
way up in the breeze.
Another small gust as the wind starts to thrust
it high above the trees.

Oh, I would love to be up above
the houses and the crowds.
I could see everything and feel like a king
high up in the clouds.

Floating on air with the wind in my hair,
flying without any fear,
I'd see my school looking so small
and wish it would disappear.

It's time for me to go home for tea
and I feel a kind of sorrow.
So I pull in the kite. That's it for the night,
but will I be back tomorrow?

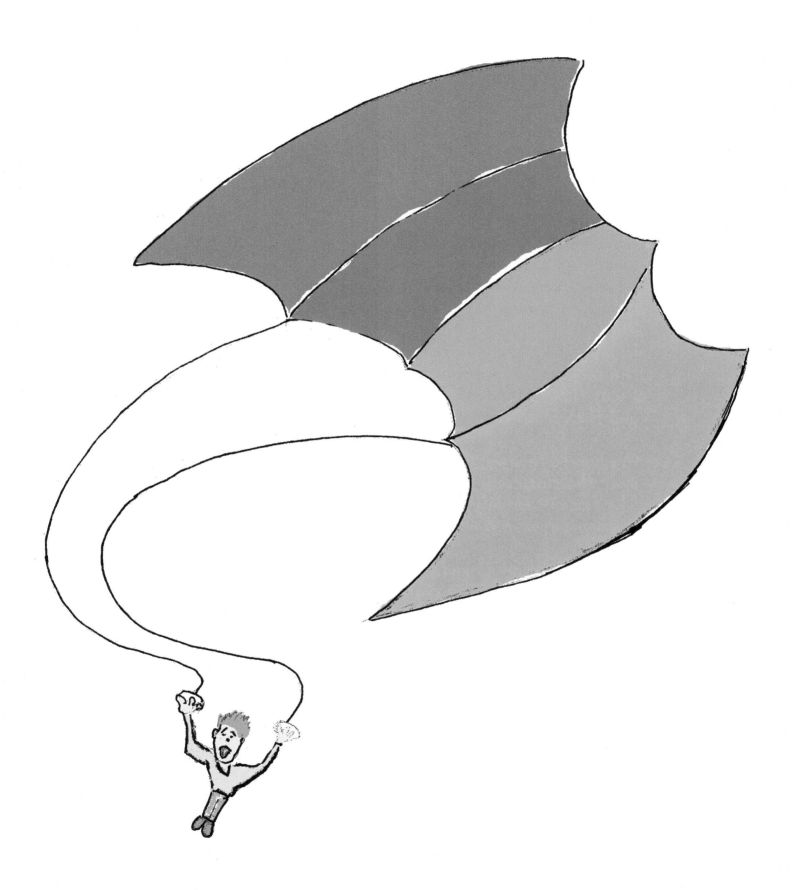

My Pet Mouse

I once kept a mouse in my pocket.
Sometimes I'd take it to school.
Nobody knew that I'd got it
for I think it's against the school rules.

I thought that maybe I'd mention
what happened the other day.
I'd landed up with detention,
because my mouse got away.

I was sitting there in the classroom,
the teacher had her back to the class.
I was thinking it would be break soon
and then it all happened so fast.

My mouse thought it would take an excursion
over the classroom floor.
The lesson suddenly took a diversion;
everyone took a run for the door.

The girls screamed and all started prancing,
the teacher stood on a chair,
the mouse, I'm afraid, kept on advancing
and teacher started pulling her hair.

Tables and chairs all went flying;
the other boys thought it was fun.
Some of the girls they were crying,
but anything is better than sums.

Now I guess that I've learned my lesson,
though it gave my teacher a turn,
but I have another confession:
in my pocket I got a slow worm!

My Pet Snail

I used to own a garden snail
and I named him Trevor.
I used to teach him little tricks,
in fact, he was quite clever.
Sometimes when my friends came round
we would have a laugh.
They would bring their own snails and found
and we would race them down the path.
These races were quite slow you know,
in fact, they could take hours.
Sometimes they'd take a little detour
and eat some of the flowers.
Dad was not so keen on that
and I should not let that happen
for snails found in his garden
he'd make sure that they were flattened.
And so I kept him safe and sound
since it's really not my wish,
you see Trevor is my friend
and I don't want him squished.

Sometimes we'd go on picnics,
we'd have a real good time.
He'd climb up and down my hands and he
would leave a trail of slime.
He'd eat the lettuce in my sandwich.
To me that was alright.
In any case a lettuce
is something I don't like.

I'd take him to the seaside
with a bucket and a spade.
It was difficult to lose him,
for the slimy trail that he made.
One day I thought I'd lost him.
I very nearly cried.
I thought that he'd been washed away
by the incoming tide.
But I need not have worried.
He was safe and sound,
hiding with the picnic things
with a salad that he'd found.

Now Dad liked growing vegetables
and some flowers too
but he didn't like the snails around
as they left a trail of goo.
They ate up all his strawberries
so he has started this embargo
on anything related to
what he would call escargot.
On a quest to hunt them down my dad
often would prevail
a ruthless long vendetta,
against these helpless snails.
He tried everything he'd heard of,
hot up on their trail
coffee grounds, and pellets,
and a pint of ale.
One sad day it happened,
Trevor found the strawberry patch,
but Dad that moment came along
and so Trevor was dispatched.

Nightmares

Last night I had a nightmare.
It really was upsetting.
I dreamt of all the homework
that I keep on getting.

Science, maths, geography
are subjects I don't like,
a pile of homework for me to do
almost every night.

I wish I didn't have to
always go to school.
I'd throw the homework on the fire,
now wouldn't that be cool!

Mum and Dad keep saying,
it will pay off in the end,
that one day I'll be leaving school,
but I can't wait 'till then.

English, French and German
drive me up the wall.
I can't wait until the day
when I'll be leaving school.

Paper Planes

When you're making paper planes
fold down the paper and take aim.
With your eye and fingers just
hold it steady before you thrust.

Just be careful what you use
with the paper that you choose.
Not too heavy, something light
and you will get a better flight.

I must admit there is an art
to folding down the perfect dart.
Make the wings a little wider
and you will have the perfect glider.

Little effort needs applying
across the room, just watch it flying,
and if it meets with no resistance
it can travel quite a distance.

It's very hard to plan its route
but sometimes it might loop the loop,
but mostly goes just anywhere
tracing circles in the air.

As long as there is lots of space,
a friend, and you can have a race.
Even have a little bet
on who has got the fastest jet?

Thought that I would make a mention
bringing this to your attention.
Just be mindful as you throw
making sure of where they go.

Origami is the name
of this very ancient game.
Whether old or if you're young,
the idea is just to have some fun.

Please Take Me to the Circus Dad

Please take me to the circus Dad!
I've heard that it's in town.
I'd like to see the acrobats,
the elephants and clowns.
I'll promise I'll be good Dad,
my homework is all done,
I've tidied up my room
and did the washing-up for Mum.

Please take me to the circus!
You promised that you would.
You said that you'd think about it
if I promised to be good.
There is a team of trapeze artists,
their act is quite a dare.
They don't use a safety harness
as they go flying through the air.

Please take me to the circus Dad
or it will be too late!
If you haven't got the tickets
you can get them at the gate.
The clowns are well worth seeing,
they really are so funny.
I laugh so much that sometimes,
I have to hold my tummy.

My friend who went there last week
said he liked it too.
He thought that the best bit
was when the elephant did a poo!
If we don't get those tickets
the trouble is I fear
we'll miss the chance to go and so,
we'll have to wait until next year.

Rabbit on

My little rabbit has a very silly habit.
The other day she nearly ran away.
Next door there is this geezer,
says he has room in his freezer.
If I want to, he would let my rabbit stay.

My neighbour keeps on joking.
He says he's always hoping
one day my rabbit would come round for tea.
Though it sounded kind, what he really had in mind,
you see, he has a rabbit recipe.

Now I don't think it's funny to joke about my bunny;
I believe it really isn't fair!
I have got my own back and kidnapped his old cat,
which is now sleeping
indoors on my chair.

Santa Came a-Calling

Santa came a-calling,
but Daddy wasn't there.
He'd popped out for a minute,
it really isn't fair.
He came into my bedroom
with a big white beard.
In a deep voice said, "Hello!"
But I wasn't scared.

Daddy won't believe it,
he'll say I dreamt it all
when I go and tell him
that Santa came to call.
Why can't Daddy be here
on an occasion such as this?
Instead, it is a moment that
Daddy has to miss.

He said, "I'll be five minutes",
but still he's not come back.
Oh, hurry up please Daddy,
here's Santa with his sack.
Whatever Daddy is doing
I'm not really sure?
I hope he's not much longer,
he only went next door.

Now Santa's left some presents
at the bottom of my bed.
He said "Goodbye 'till next year!"
then kissed me on the head.
This could have been the moment,
that Daddy and I could share,
when Santa came a-calling,
but Daddy was not there.

Scrumping

We'd sometimes go scrumping,
my brother and me,
filling our pockets
as we climbed apple trees.
Sometimes we'd find pears,
greengages or plums.
My brother kept lookout –
the farmer might come!

We lived in the country
on the borders of Kent.
Many a summer
we'd happily spent.
Kent is the Garden
of England, they say,
with orchards of apples
where we often played.

It's where we'd go scrumping,
my brother and I
when we'd take home the proceeds
for Mum's apple pies.
I loved those green apples
and climbing trees,
in search of the summer
while scraping our knees.

The best kind of apples
we often found
were not on the tree
but the ones on the ground.
Dad said it's naughty
to pick from the tree
so we'd pick up the windfalls.
That was ok with me.

The Divorce

My mum and dad
are getting divorced.
I'm a pig in the middle –
a dilemma, of course.

But nobody notices.
Nobody cares.
Sometimes I wonder
if they know I'm there.

There are arguments daily
that just get me down.
It's no wonder my friends
just won't come around.

I don't understand it
and want them to know
that I love them dearly
and don't want Dad to go.

I can remember
when life was more fun,
now it looks like I'm losing
a dad or a mum.

By compromising,
a solution is found,
but one or two ground rules
must be laid down.

Mondays to Fridays
with Mum I will stay
and Dad at the weekends
is the best way.

It's not what I wanted,
but what can I do?
There is no turning back now
the divorce has gone through.

The Enterprising Mouse

Now there was a mouse
who lived in a house
where the people who lived there were vegans.
He said if you please
they never eat cheese
it's something that they don't believe in.

Oh, what I would do
for some nice Danish Blue
or a lovely great chunk of Caerphilly.
For a cheese connoisseur
the poor mouse was bored;
he thought that the whole thing was silly.

He had an idea,
the plan was quite clear.
"At last," he said, "I think I've got it!
Everybody agrees
that the moon's made of cheese,
so I'll build myself a small rocket."

Now as everyone knows
on the Blue Peter shows
the things they make are fantastic.
You need a small piece of tubing
held on till it's glued in,
some string and some sticky back plastic.

His rocket was built
with Blue Peter's help
and soon it was time for the countdown.
He said his farewells
to his family and pals
and all those who gathered around.

One has to admit
this mouse has some grit,
to take on such an endeavour.
For it's on his return
no doubt we will learn
if the moon really is made of Cheddar.

76

The Seaside

When the summer is here I like to be
spending the day down by the sea,
exploring the rock pools, collecting some crabs
or playing beach ball with my brother and Dad.

We'd watch the seagulls, see how they'd fly,
appearing to hang there, up in the sky.
The wind seemed to catch them, on a warm breeze
and gently blow them right out to sea.

The cool waves would wash and tingle our toes
as in and out the tide it would flow.
We often stood there, up to our knees.
Oh, we enjoyed it, down by the sea.

Then maybe later we might decide
to hire out a boat or a nice donkey ride.
There would be Punch and Judy, perhaps an ice cream.
When fingers are sticky just lick them clean.

Sometime sandcastles we often made
with turrets and steep walls built with bucket and spade.
Around the outside we dig a moat,
fill it with water where little boat's float.

Thinking about it brings nice memories
of lovely hot summers down by the sea.
So roll along summer so we can once again
enjoy the warm sunshine instead of cold winter rain.

The Snowman

I look out of the window
and saw there was snow.
If the school closes
we won't have to go.
Maybe after breakfast
I'll ask if we can
go out in the garden
and build a snowman.

My brother can help me,
that's if he likes
and perhaps when we've finished
we'll have a snow fight.
Mum's got a carrot
to use as a nose
and Dad's got some old hats –
we'll use one of those.

We've nearly finished
and it's looking quite good.
We will give him some arms
with some old bits of wood.
We will finish it off
with this funny old scarf
then Mum calls out the window,
"It's time for a bath!"

Dad videoed us.
We can later admire
the snowman we made
while we sit round the fire.
It's so exciting,
I wish I was sure,
when we wake up tomorrow,
it would snow a bit more.

Up in the Attic

Up in the attic where nobody goes,
there is an old tea chest full of old clothes.
There are old hats and trousers, maybe a silk dress,
a whole wardrobe in fact, up there, more or less.
There's a long wooden sword for a knight in full armour
or an old straw hat that would look good on a farmer.
There are outfits for doctors and nurses of course
and even what might be a pantomime horse.

On days when it's cold, or if there is rain
Mum lets us play there so we make it a game.
Imagination, that's all it took,
we would play out a story from a film or a book.
Long lost explorers looking for treasure,
or maybe become lords and ladies of leisure,
cowboys and indians, or knights of the realm,
or cut-throated pirates, with Blackbeard at the helm.

So much fun and it just never ends
and we'd like to share it with you my dear friends.
So if you're not too busy, you could have a go,
get some old costumes and put on a show.
Progress in this venture need not be impeded;
get Mum and Dad clothes that are no longer needed,
some useful props and put in a chest.
Your imagination can do all the rest.

Yo-Yos

My brother's got a yo-yo
and no one that I know though
can play it quite like him.
The tricks that he can master,
slow and sometimes faster,
as he puts it in a spin.

He does some special tricks
with a counter-clockwise flick
as it takes a different route.
You'd see him flick his wrist
as he gives another twist.
It would fly out in a loop
then he'd make a forward pass
and make it spin real fast.
That's called a Power Throw.
There's another called a Spinner,
which shows he's no beginner.
There's quite a few you know.

There's the Flying Saucer
the Breakaway and Sleeper
and many he can show.
Though the one they call Trapeze
fills me full of quiet unease
but I'm gonna have a go.

PAGE AFTER PAGE

MAKING INDIVIDUAL BOOKS AND JOURNALS

FRANCES PICKERING

I dedicate this book to
my mother Norah Jameson
who got me stitching and
to my grandaughters
Grace and Daisy Hodgson.

I have taught and enjoyed embroidery and Textiles for many years, but over the last few years making stitched and illustrated books and teaching people how to make them has become the main focus of my work. I am inspired to make books on many different subjects but nature and the countryside are my first loves. I love experimenting and I try to use many unorthodox methods to decorate and fill the books I make. I gain great pleasure from the fact that I have made the complete book. I recycle as many things as possible and strive to turn them into something of worth. The purpose of this book is to inspire people to try to make their own individual and personal books.

'Gardens... furnished with many rare Simples, do singularly delight, when in them a man doth behold a flourishing shew of Summer beauties in the midst of Winters force, and a goodly spring of flours, when abroad a leaf not to be scene.'
    JOHN GERARD

3.

WHY BOOKS

What is a book and what is it for?
The dictionary says " A BOOK CONSISTS OF A NUMBER OF PIECES OF PAPER, USUALLY WITH WORDS OR PICTURES PRINTED ON THEM, WHICH ARE FASTENED TOGETHER AND FIXED INSIDE A COVER OF STRONGER PAPER OR CARDBOARD.
This can be a starting point.........

All sorts of paper can be used, also fabric treated with various media and stitched into layers.....

St Thomas Becket, Fairfield...

Mysterious Romney Marsh

'Smuggling..... derived from the Saxon 'smugan', meaning to creep about with secrecy......

A finished book can have a life and worth of its own.....

Of course words can be used..............
But also try beads, buttons, pressed flowers, drawings, stitch

and a host of other things......

WORDS

Colour, texture and form is very important when making
a book.........
Try using recycled materials.........it is rewarding to
start with unpromising materials and then turn them
into something of worth.......

CONSTRUCTION METHODS CAN BE KEPT VERY SIMPLE

Photos can be
stitched and stuck
down on the
page. Maps
can be dyed with
tea and stitched.

Books are unique to the person who makes them.

GETTING STARTED

Sketchbooks can be a very good way to start and don't have to be full of drawings...... paper & fabric samples can also be added.... Sketchbooks can get you in the mood for starting your book.....

daisy
daisy

daisy

daisy

colours ran dry between colours—

The greater wild daisy is a wound herb of good respect, often used in those salves and drinks that are for wounds'.

CULPEPPERS HERBAL

daisy cut from Pelmet Vilene painted with water-based dyes and green pen......

Daisy chain cut from pelmet vilene — along pages.

Daisy chain to be cut out down the side of pages.

'Of all the flowers in the mead

Then love I most those flowers white

while and redde.

Such that men call daisies in our town.

CHAUCER.

Samples can be stuck or stitched in

Edges of pages or cover can be cut to shape ?

Crushed daisies can be used for brushes and stencils ...... folklore.

cut out

DAISY DAISY

Could try making pages from layers of plastic .... not bad to draw on.

'To see a world in a grain of sand
And heaven in a wild flower
Hold infinity in the palm of your hand
And eternity in an hour.

William Blake.

7.

'But one, the
Sai   of

Small

8.

... as morn, of many a hue,
... ushing clouds ... through da...
... in dew

Sketchbooks are a place
to keep your thoughts and
ideas before you start...

bleach on paper ↓

bleach added to
transfer dye.

transfer dye onto pelmet
vilene - added
colour & pen.

Make lists........ write objectives, idea
materials to collect and maybe small
sketches of some of the pages, and
ideas for construction.........
Keep a small notebook for jotting
ideas down....... Think about what
you want to achieve.......

SOME IDEAS FOR TOPICS
Just a few ideas for starters!

Personal journal/diary   Gardens.
Celebrations.   A special place.
A collection of verses.
   Recipes.   Birds.
Family History   Trees.
                          Flowers.
The Seashore.   Butterflies.
   The Seasons.
                     A daily walk.
A memory book.
       And so much more......

herbs · · shells · · · flowers · · · leaves · · · trees · · · birds · · · feathers

Some people are fearful of others seeing their work. This particularly applies to drawing. A small private book can be kept for sketches until you feel more confident. This small book can also be used for your private thoughts and not for viewing by the public ....

Little books are just right for keeping in your pocket ..... in binding ....

KEEP EVERYTHING IN A BASKET.

When commencing a book, keep all the relevant materials in one basket or box that you can carry around with you. It can be more of a challenge to limit the amount of items in your container. It can make you more creative!

11.

It can help to do some research before making a book.

Collect second-hand books, go to the library, use the internet and keep a collection of quotes that might be useful.

Friends and family can be very helpful and will often collect things for you.

Keep all these things together........

If you don't want to draw what you see ....cut out images, use photographs & stitch.....

LOOK OUT OF THE WINDOW.....

'Pack, clouds, away, and welcome day'.....

Thomas Heywood

It is helpful to have a small notebook to hand. The best ideas come in the most unlikely places.....

Sometimes the smallest thing can inspire you to make a special book for yourself.

Handwriting is often something that people feel bothered about when adding text to their pages. They don't think their writing is good enough to be displayed. Writing in a book can be integral to the way the book looks. Words on a page look more spontaneous if they are in your own hand.

...DISGUISING MISTAKES.

- Print and stitch....
- Cover with interesting paper.
- Stitch onto fabric or paper and stick over mistake.
- Cut the mistake out and use the remaining hole as a window.
- Fold the paper over and stick down.......

If you don't want to write the text yourself, you can cut words out a newspaper or magazine. You could also use the computer. Words can be left out altogether.......

...DON'T BE FRIGHTENED OF MAKING MISTAKES. ...... THERE IS USUALLY A WAY TO COVER THEM UP ....

13.

Gather together in one place all you need, before you start........

lace edging

Gold edging on collar...

embroidery

always have my sight.

I cannot have

have said before

Cupid with his

deadly dart

Doth wound my he...

(A Midsumm...

14.

remembere[d]
[g]reat bea[uty]
with a ne[edle]

[NEED]LEWORK
ENCYCLOPAE[DIA]

looks not with the eyes,
ith the mind,
Shakespeare

15.

INSPIRATIONS

Two shapely leaves will first unfold,
Then on a smooth, elastic stem,
The verdant bud shall go to gold
And open in a diadem.

It helps to choose something personal to you to start with. If you are enthusiastic about your subject, you are more likely to complete your book......

Look at your surroundings; precious memories or a collection you might have started.

BOOKS COME IN MANY SHAPES AND SIZES ..... DECIDE WHAT IS RIGHT FOR YOUR PARTICULAR THEME......

Stitching adds interest and structure to the page.....

A QUOTE MIGHT BE JUST WHAT YOU NEED TO GET STARTED.....

The original is then simplified to be used as a repeat pattern block ....

16.

Water based dyes can produce vibrant colours ....

Printing block made from press print ....

Book cover made from calico printed with water based dyes. The cover was then covered with acrylic wax ....

Tulip print made with PZKUT block

Two shapely leaves will first unfold ....

Cover made using pelmet vilene and transfer dyes

The quote from the previous page was stitched on the cover ....

17.

An old collection of embroidery and needlework items can be a wonderful topic to centre a book around... It is a great way to keep a collection together especially if it is a family treasure!!

Pages can be decorated by painting them with a mixture of strong tea and watercolour... Sandwich lace between two pages that have been painted and iron until dry...... Lace prints are then left as a background......

stitch on empty cards to add interest...

Pages could be made of calico instead of paper......

small treasures in calico or paper envelopes

SNAP SIZE 2
MADE IN ENGLAND

MILADI
TRADE MARK
MENDING COMPACT
MADE IN ENGLAND

NEEDLES

J. DEWHURST & SONS Ltd
SYLKO
FAST DYE
10 YARDS
D. 111
BRIGHT NAVY

MADE IN GREAT BRITAIN
ANCHOR
COLOUR S 2938

Pages from a sketchbook or notebook can be incorporated into the book you are working on. Suitable colour thread can be used to blend the whole page together......

'Beautiful children of the woods and fields' Robert Nicoll.

The Song Thrush has arrow-shaped marks on its front...

Within a thick and spreading
hawthorn bush
That overhung a molehill
large and round,
I heard from morn to morn
a merry thrush.
John Clare

19.

BIRD

Within my garden, rides a Bird
Upon a single Wheel Whose name
Whose spokes a dizzy Music make
As 'twere a travelling Mill —
EMILY DICKINSON

A small lively bird with
a blue cap ringed with
white ....
'Bobbing on Willow branches, blue and
Acrobatic blue tits swing and sway
in careful somersaults and neat
Giving gymnastic gyrations
pulling dexterity
Aerial spray.'

BIRDS IN OUR
CHARING GARDEN
KENT

'Brave bluetit, white-cheeked like a painted toy'
PHOEBE HESKETH

BLUE TIT (FEMALE)
PLAYER'S CIGARETTES

Blue Tit, Coal Tit and Great Tit
all come into the garden .....

taps loudly with its bill

sociable birds with quick,
Jenny movements .....

The blue tits come to see us
now ..... free hung

Blue Tit .....
A shorter, more
triangular bill
smaller than a
finch s.

G.

20.

4th October...
Mike and Gwen's House in Spain.

and look wonderful...

lad

I and shall preserve my youth Barickes Herbal

The grapes are over......
the leaves are the most beautiful colour...

Mall

The leaves on the Lemon Tree smell like freshly squeezed Lemons!

this FROM MONPA at
It was Gwen and Mikes Wedding Anniversary today......

I find verdant olives round the year' flourish Homer....

worked in the garden most of the day .... lovely and hot!!!

MARY FOR REMEMBER

TO MAKE A COVER

The cover is the first thing to be seen and needs to create a good impression so the reader will want to look inside...

As your book is probably going to be looked at frequently it needs to be robust enough to withstand being handled and even tolerate being put in a pocket or bag........

Pelmet Vilene is an ideal choice for a book cover as it doesn't fray and is easy to cut and fold....(see page) 52.

Pelmet Vilene painted with waterbased dyes and when dry coated with acrylic wax........

Image drawn on paper with a candle. Transfer dyes applied over the top and ironed off onto pelmet vilene. Right hand image worked into with coloured pencils....

22.

1.

2.

3.

4.

5.

6.

7.

Cloth coloured with Transfer dye and coloured pencils.
Machine stitched....

Different surfaces using Pelmet Vilene.

1. Lace dyed with tea and bonded to vilene.

2. Lace dyed with water based dyes.

3. Coloured pencils and acrylic wax.

4. water based dyes. printed with a cork and decorated with metallic pen.

5. Acrylic paint. coated with wax and decorated with PVA glue and treasure gold.

6. Acrylic paints and soldering iron.

7. Acrylic paints and metallic pens..

Transfer dyes and pelmet Vilene are an excellent combination when making covers......

Transfer dyes are quick and easy to use and pelmet Vilene does not fray and can be cut and burnt very easily...... The paper used to transfer your design can be coated with Acrylic wax and can then be used as the lining for your cover.........

Interesting effects can be achieved by applying bleach to transfer dyed paper and then ironing off...

Shapes can be cut out of the Vilene and applied...

Cover printed using transfer dyes with added coloured pencil!

24.

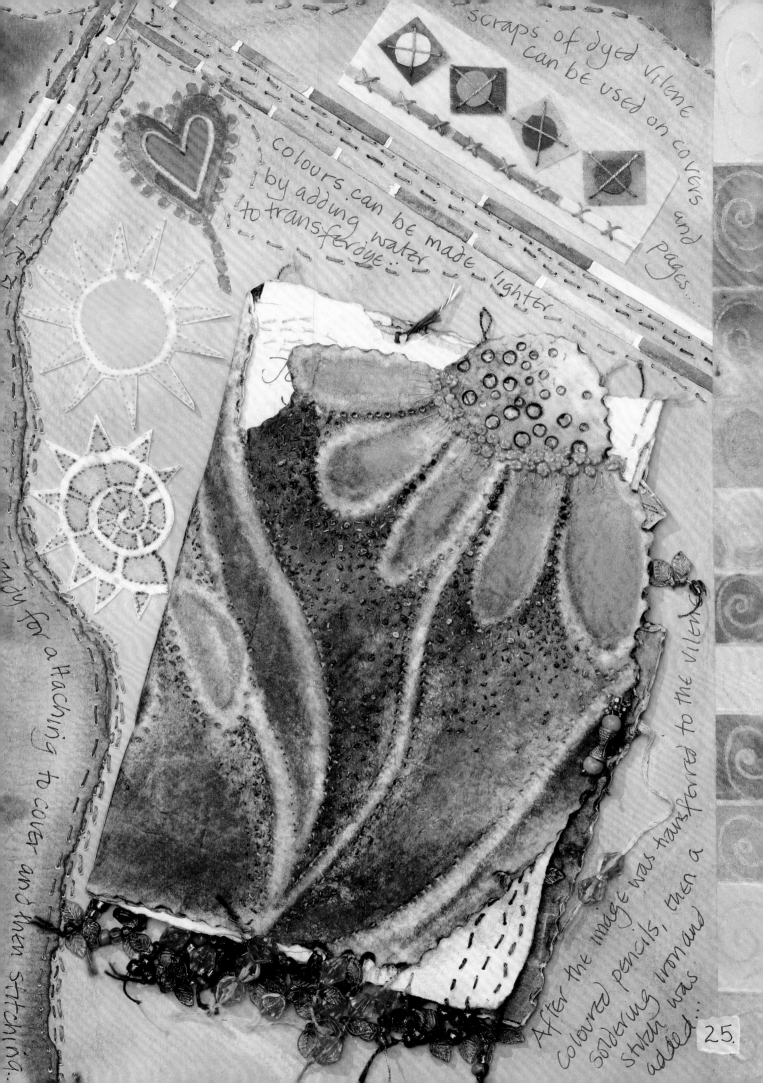

scraps of dyed vilene can be used on covers and pages...

colours can be made lighter by adding water to transfer dye...

...dy for a Haching to cover and then stitching...

After the image was transferred to the vilene coloured pencils, then a soldering iron and stitch was added...

25.

Ah. Sunflower

Wonderful backgrounds can be achieved with Transfer Dyes, a great starting point for stitch..

26.

'Tis moonlight, Summer

Moonlig

...man can become a neat sew...

among the woodlands shady

nooks the primrose

wanly comes

'Live Primrose then, and thrive
With thy true number five'
JOHN DONNE

Many techniques can be
used to make books.....

29.

MAKING PAGES

- Select the paper you are going to use. (see opposite)

- Make the pages to fit the cover, cut or tear to size.

- The pages need to be slightly smaller than the cover.

- Make one page first and then use it as a template.

- For the end paper you need a piece the same size as the cover.

- If you tear the pages, you needn't be so precise.

wall paper lining

wallpaper lining with water based dyes...

paper coloured

paper coloured

cartridge paper

lining paper coloured with tea.

Brown paper coloured with water based dyes...

PAGES

good paper for

SUITABLE PAPER FOR

30.

TO COLOUR PAGES.

Lay a piece of polythene or a dustbin liner on a work surface.

Choose colours carefully as they mix on the paper.

Put colours in small jars or pots.

Lay down on the polythene the first piece of paper. Paint in broad strokes a mixture of colours covering the whole sheet.

Turn the sheet over and repeat the process on the other side.

Lay the next sheet of paper across the first at an angle while it is still wet. Colour this sheet exactly the same as the first, turning it over and making sure all of the sheet is coloured.

Repeat this process until you have a pile of all of your pages including your end paper.

Leave for at least thirty minutes, the longer you leave the pages the better they get.

CARRY ON WORKING INTO YOUR PAGES IF YOU WANT TO:

• Brush over with gesso and rub back with a baby wipe or similar.

• Knock back the colour with a wash of tea to create an antique effect.

• Over print with bleach* or paint

• Work into a specific area using crayons or paint to lighten or darken or enhance

• Apply colour along the edges of pages......

* SEE PAGE 55 FOR SAFETY ADVICE

shapes, patterns or colours.

31.

'She bewitched me
With such a sw...
I knew not wh...
And when I fou...

In Eastern lands they talk in flowers
And they tell in a garland their loves and cares.
Each blossom that blooms in their garden bowers
On its leaves a mystic language bears.

James Gates Percival.

32.

Experiment with a variety of papers and colouring techniques to make pages...

We are blushing Roses,
Bending with our fulness,
Midst our close-capped sister buds.

Warming the green coolness!

...gh Hunt.

...ord but look
and love awhile,
'Twas but one
half-hour,
Then to resist I had
no will,
And now I have
no power!'
THOMAS OTWAY.

'O that...

'Of all the flou...
Than love I most
these floures
white and rede
Soch that men
callen daisies in
our toun'......
CHAUCER.

33.

DECORATING PAGES

Filling a book is a very personal expression of your feelings towards the subject matter. There is a great deal of satisfaction to be had by working in your book and filling it up......

You don't have to start with the first page if that is too daunting. Find a page further in the book with some interesting marks that inspire you to get going.

Fit quotes in the book as appropriate.

Progress from page to page, trying to get the right balance.

SHAPING THE EDGE OF THE PAGE CREATES IMPACT AND INTEREST.

There are many printing blocks on the market. The secret is to use them creatively and develop your own style......

It is important that the pages sit happily next to each other thus creating a flow which says something about the subject. Making the book up first means you would work on the book as a complete whole......

Beads, found objects, tags, luggage labels even a small book can be hong from the bottom edges of pages or even the cover.

Start with a Knot and then thread on the bead. do a back stitch into the bead and then carry on threading on beads until you are ready to stitch on the page. Do another back stitch into the last bead. (see diagram) ....

RUNNING STITCH WORKS ALMOST ANYWHERE ...

TRY DIFFERENT STITCHES ON THE EDGES OF THE PAGES......

— back stitch

— back stitch

— back stitch
— Knot.

Remember when stitching pages, there are a few things to think of first..
Stitching will show on the other side so make sure it is interesting to look at ....

Strips of fabric with added stitches or adornments, can all be stuck over the back to hide stitching

Use books as bees

Use flowers

The darkly shining salt sea drops
Streamed as the waves clashed
The beach, with all its   orga
Pealing again, prolonged the

A BED OF ROSES

I WILL MAKE THEE

'I will make thee beds of roses
With a thousand fragrant posies
A cap of flowers, and a kirtle
Embroidery all with leaves of myrtle

Christopher M

The Dandelion is a   utiful plant

'Dandelio
a happy o
to spinach
leaves shoul
cooked first
take longer
spinach... Se
hot with butter
and a squeeze
m juice

folk lore has it that the

Bleach can be used to
great effect on darker
pages...

36.

shore;

JOHN DAVIDSON.

of breaths it takes

a dandelion globe that has gone

off all the seeds

The silver ha
the mass
hair
me
will not kiss my sweet
lover's flower.

37.

Bleach can be used on pages to great effect......
If your pages are dark you can pick out highlights.

bleached out

Try drawing, painting or printing with bleach. Dry as quickly as possible. Dry as quickly as possible. They can then be coloured. When the bleached areas are dry they can bleach back to show different effects printing to the background colours according to you have used.

GREAT CARE MUST BE TAKEN WHEN USING BLEACH. (SEE PAGE 55.)

Torn paper painted with ? and veins

Drawn with bleach and filled in with bleach

38.

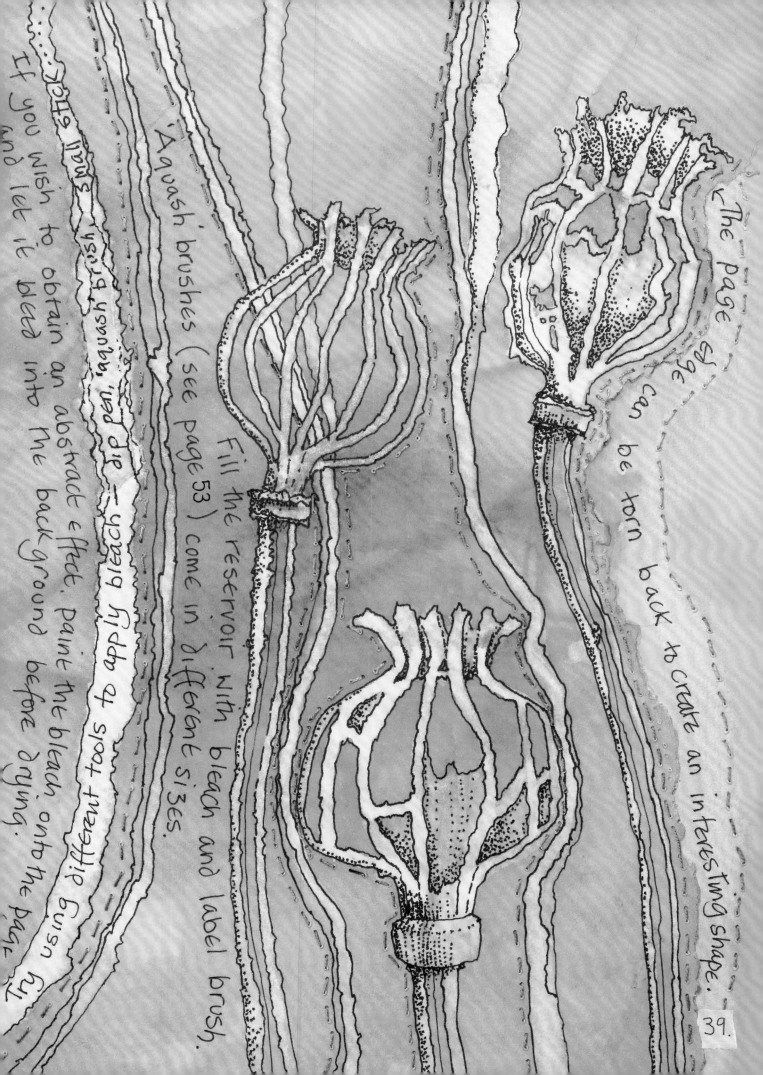

The page edge can be torn back to create an interesting shape.

Fill the reservoir with bleach and label brush.

'Aquash' brushes (see page 53) come in different sizes.

different tools to apply bleach — dip pen, 'aquash' brush, small stick

If you wish to obtain an abstract effect. Paint the bleach onto the page and let it bleed into the background before drying.

Shapes can be drawn onto the page as a background – try using 'Aquawax' or a candle...

Sewing beads along the edge of a page is time consuming but can add that extra 'sparkle' on the appropriate page. Beads must be small or the page will get marked and will not shut.

The 'Aquawax' or candle needs to be 'ironed off' using a piece of brown paper on top. The image can then be written on........

Continually the Ocean's face

Delightful would it be to me – from a rock pinnacle to trace

St Columba

of Iona

When candle is used directly onto the page the colour underneath shows...

Papers that have been treated with transfer dye and ironed off may have a small amount of residue dye left on them. The papers can be ironed onto your pages to give weak images.

The original papers can be cut and torn to also be used on the pages. Part of the paper can be used for borders, they can be worked into with crayons, paints etc and painted with Acrylic Wax to give a contrast to the matt pages.

If you cut out holes, or have doors or windows in the page something interesting should be shown behind it or on the next page ......

If you have a lot of stitching .... pieces of artwork can be stuck together

Round and round we go ......

pages on the page or

Remember to change the scale of your image with the size of book.

ASSEMBLING AND FASTENINGS

your fastening should be pratical but fit with the overall design

old linen buttons can be coloured and waxed

Button on the back fastened with a cord....

Buttons can be made from pelmet vilene or old buttons rubbed with teasie Gold....

Fastening should be attached before making the book up ....

Small books, tags or beads can be hung from the cover or used as a bookmark.......

DAISY DAISY

42.

stitch spine carefully to achieve a neat finish......

... TO ASSEMBLE YOUR BOOK...

• Lay paper/fabric for the lining and the cover right sides together.
• Draw around lining and cover and cut out ......
• Using PVA glue, stick lining to cover.. Leave overnight if possible..
• Lay cover flat and pages on top. line up folds. Large paperclips or similar help to hold everything together..
• Make an uneven number of holes in the fold at regular intervals...
• Go through pages and cover.
Using medium/thick thread starting at the centre go in and out of the holes. Thread needle through last stitch and tie off......

Linings can be so plain or decorative so you like ....

When your book is finished, do up the fastening, lay it down on a blanket or towel and place a weight or pile of books on it overnight.

Wherever you start stitching the spine, start on the outside .... if you want to hang beads etc from the spine, start on the spine is where you will finish.

Wherever you start stitching the spine is where you will finish.

43.

Life is just a bowl of cherries

Don't take it serious; life's so mysterious!....

44.

The fastening of the book should
be an integral part of the design.

45.

TRAVEL JOURNALS

when there is nothing else.... a biro works for a quick sketch....

Buttons from the market.....

LEAVE SPACE FOR PHOTOGRAPHS

TRAVEL KIT

Colouring medium of your own choice.

Small plastic pot with lid (for water.)

A couple of paint brushes.

A couple of drawing pens and pencils.

Glue stick.

Small pair of scissors.

Some threads and a few needles.

Your journal you have made to fill.

* The above items and your book should fit into a small bag.

do quick drawings of wild flowers. look them up when you get home......

MUSÉES

TRY USING DIFFERENT SURFACES TO DRAW AND WRITE TO

CORKS MAKE VERY GOOD PORTABLE PRINTING BLOCKS.

↑ BLOTTING PAPER
↘ GESSO ON PAPER.

HOLIDAY BROCHURE
↓

Travel journals need to be something you can carry around with you without being cumbersome. Collect pictures, maps, quotes and descriptive passages to use in your book before you go. This with some stitch and colour will get you started. Try and fill your book on a daily basis. Extra items can be added when you get home.

Le centre équestre
FRAYSSINET LE GELAT en direction
nche de Périgord (10 km)

47.

The Tourist Information Office is often a good starting point. They generally have a wealth of brochures, postcards, posters and local maps. These can be torn or cut up, treated with tea or your colouring medium and pasted or sewn in your book. Stamps from other countries always seem more interesting than our own – they can look wonderful stuck along the edges of pages and stitched into your book you can, or draw straight into old linen buttons coloured with watercolour. They also come with their own glue! collect tickets, labels, stamps and menus . . . . . . on other paper and stick it with in

If you want to draw

Carvings on a church door

with acrylic wax (see page 52).

Behind. paint. pencil and rub

it was so juicy I had to eat it outside

breakfast

40 **LIN EXTRA** DÉPOSÉE
FIL
CARTE ALSACIENNE
DE **FRANCE**
LYON · COMINES

traveller
ARTISTIQUE (Mar

48.

Filling the journal while
on are on holiday
means you absorb
the sights, colours
and atmosphere and
record them in your
book.

If you don't want
to draw, you can keep
your book as a diary.

Spend a week in the Lot valley
In South West France.

MAKE A
COLLAGE WITH SCRAPS
OF PAPER OR TAKE A RUBBING.
ADD STITCH TO CREATE TEXTURE.

The sun is/was optimistic as there was not much of it !!!

VACANCE...

MALBERNAT
B&B HOLIDAYS

WANDE

...es of violets
...ong the road
...e way to Cazals

Pigeonniers can be on columns on top of a barn adorned with half-timbering or a turret.

The pigeons were kept for food and their droppings were a strong fertiliser...

THE HEAD GARDENER'S CHOICE

HELIGAN

CLARKIA
Double Mixed

Annual. Sow in situ in early spr...
or autumn & thin out as requir...
Protect autumn sowings with...
cloche. Requires fertile, well-dr...
soil in full sun/partial shad...
H30cm/1ft.

The Lost Gardens of
HELIGAN

Pentewan, St. Austell, Cornwall, P...
Tel: 01726 845100 Fax: 01726 6...

THE HELFORD RIVER...

The Helford is a ria – a drowned river valley.

Discover the Coast

A varied selection of Travel Journals...

50.

We went on the ferry fro...

'Those fraternal Four of Borrowdale, joined in one solemn and capacious grove'.....
WILLIAM WORDSWORTH

Borrowdale's oak woods once formed part of a temperate rainforest —
"The Borrowdale Rambler" runs south to Grange and Seatoller.....

stopped the car so we could walk and smell the herbs.....

wonderful colours, sounds and smells .....

51.

MATERIALS.

ACRYLIC WAX.

Acrylic wax is resistant to heat and water. It can be applied on any porous surface making it feel like it is coated with beeswax. It can be applied with a brush over most mediums from water-colour to fabric paint providing a seal, enhancing the colour and improving the feel of the item. When dry it can be buffed to a shine. You can also mix colour and powdered pigments with it. Brushes can be be washed out in water.

PELMET VILENE.

Pelmet Vilene is generally used by people making soft furnishings. It is a stiff synthetic material which mainly comes in white. Because it's synthetic it melts with the application of a soldering iron. As an alternative try experimenting with calico, thick cotton etc.

GLUE

For sticking photographs, dried flowers, pieces of paper, tickets etc onto the pages of books a simple glue stick is useful, but PVA is longer lasting. Use PVA for larger applications.........

PENS.

There are many pens on the market that are available for use. Sketching pens are waterproof and lightfast. They come in various widths. For the text black or sepia work well but dark green or blue can also be effective. Occasionally white or gold can be used. Find what is best for you....

POWDERED WATERCOLOUR.

It can be mixed with cold water to make strong vibrant transparent colours. It can be sprinkled onto wet or dry surfaces and worked into. Mixed with other waterbased mediums such as acrylic wax, it creates interesting effects.

DYES.

The easiest way to use dyes whilst making books is to use a dye based water colour palette (such as KOH-I-NOOR). Leftover dyes from fabric and thread dyeing sessions can be used. Left over dyes can be kept in jam jars.

AQUASH BRUSHES

Aquash brushes have synthetic tips, come in three sizes and have a plastic reservoir for holding liquid. Bleach can be put in the reservoir. Label it well.

TREASURE GOLD

Treasure Gold is a metallic wax paste that comes in a wide range of gorgeous colours. It can be rubbed on with a finger, brush or soft cloth. It can be buffed to a shine when it is dry. Use it for highlighting small areas of raised design or on page edges. Care should be taken not to use it too much — you can have too much of a good thing.

SOLDERING IRON

The smaller models made for model makers are ideal. They are available from hardware stores, model making shops and also some art and craft shops. There are also specialist websites. Most come with a handy stand for safe operation.

Great care must be taken when using the soldering iron.

BUTTONS AND BEADS.

All manner of buttons and beads and ephemera can be used to fasten books and to hang from the bottom of pages. Look on the internet, jumble sales and flea markets for interesting shapes and sizes..

TRANSFER DYES.

Transferable dye colour for fabrics
Images produced on thin paper
can be transferred
by ironing onto
synthetics or
synthetic mix fabrics.
The dye powder can be made up to the desired
strength. Transfer dye is excellent for use on
pelmet vilene for book covers.

SAFETY ADVICE.

I cannot stress strongly enough
how important it is to follow the
manufacturer's instructions when
using:
Irons, Heatguns, Hairdryers,
Soldering Irons, Bleach, Dyes.
When in doubt wear gloves
and a face mask. Work in a
well ventilated room.

Most of the materials featured
in this book are available
from ART VAN GO.
The Studios, 1 Stevenage Road
Knebworth
Hertfordshire SG3 6AN
01438 814946
e: art@artvango.co.uk.
www.artvango.co.uk.

Cotton Lavendar ....
rub crushed leaves on insect bites to ease the pain....

Feverfew ..... is a ....
can also be made into ....

'The World's a garden;
pleasures are the flowers
of fairest hues, in form
and number many...
SHAKESPEARE....

– Garden Daisy....

...SEA HOLLY......

It has been windy just beginning and th to b

Dead leaves f

for certain types of migraine old

In Ancient Gr Sea Holly was as 'eromgeraui which means to because physic used the root o the plant to red swelling

THE SIXTEENTH CENTURY HERBALIST JOHN GERARD DESCRIBED THE PLANT AS THE THISTLE OF THE SEA.

57.

ERYNGIUM

Flowers leave some of their
fragrance in the hand that
bestows them....
Chinese proverb

The flower is the poetry
of reproduction
It is the example of the
external seductiveness of
life.... Jean Giraudoux

Thank you God for most this amazing
day: for the leaping greenly spirits of trees
and a blue true dream of sky; and
for everything
which is natural which is infinite which is
E.E. Cummings....

Unkempt about those hedges blows
An English unofficial rose ......

Birds love the
Sunflower seeds

58.

the poor mans

Valerian

In the West of
It has been suggested
rat-charming that
lay more in the

g Valerian roots and
add the decoction to

poppies in all the fields

as if paint has been flung across the
is the plant of sleep and because
abundant seeds of fertility, its
folklore of plants

Corn and
Poppy
Margaret Baker

59.

I WOULD LIKE TO THANK

Viv Arthur and Kevin Mead for all their help and encouragement over the years.

My family especially Rebecca, Edward and Thomas who had to grow up with a crazy Textile Artist as a mother.

Lindsay Griffiths (who thankfully shares the same sense of humour) and Betty Parker who has been like a second Mum to me.

Pauline and John Horne for all their support and kindness.

My 'Gang of Four' - Audrey, Charlotte, Christine and Liz for sharing this fun journey with me.

Most of all my wonderful husband Jim for all his love, creativity and expertise without which this book wouldn't have got started, let alone finished.